WORDSAR
ENTALWAY
SMEANTT
OBEREAD

DON'T
TRY
THIS AT
HOME

The
Medium
is the
Message
And 50 other
Ridiculous Advertising Rules

COLOPHON

BIS Publishers
Het Sieraad
Postjesweg 1
1057 DT Amsterdam
The Netherlands
T (+) 31 (0)20-515 02 30
F (+) 31 (0)20-515 02 39
bis@bispublishers.nl
www.bispublishers.nl

ISBN 978-90-6369-215-5

Copyright © 2009 BIS Publishers

Ridiculous Design Rules is a concept developed
by Lemon Scented Tea and commissioned by
Premsela, Dutch Platform for Design and Fashion
(www.premsela.org).

Editorial Director: Anneloes van Gaalen
(www.paperdollwriting.com)
Designed by: Lilian van Dongen Torman
(www.born84.nl)

BISPUBLISHERS

The Medium is the Message

And 50 other
Ridiculous Advertising Rules

CONTENTS

INTRODUCTION

Every single day we're bombarded with a regular onslaught of advertising. The paper you read, the magazine you buy, the radio show you listen to: they all feature ads. There's product placement on TV and on the silver screen. And the moment you go online you're exposed to anything from pop-up ads to spam. And let's not forget about the public transport that is covered in slogans, and the enormous billboards and flashy neon signs that are all there in the public domain, vying for your attention. No opportunity is wasted by the ad men to grab the attention of potential customers and entice, seduce or convince them to buy a certain product, service or idea.

Not surprising then that advertising has been called the greatest art form of the 20th century, as well as the biggest evil man has ever produced. Whether or not you believe in a thing called ARTvertising or are of the opinion that advertising, along with branding and marketing, is downright diabolical, you're bound to find this book a source of inspiration.

We've collected and researched a total of 51 rules, including 'The Medium is the Message', 'Make the Logo Bigger' and that old favorite 'Sex Sells'. All the great ad men and women make an appearance, sharing their thoughts and insights. The aim in making this book was not to list all the rules that a budding copywriter or marketer needs to adhere to. Nor did we want to decide which rules are indeed ridiculous and which are valuable words of wisdom. Instead consider this book a source of comfort, joy or good old fun. After all, it's like American advertising executive Jerry Della Femina (1936) once said: "Advertising is the most fun you can have with your clothes on."

Also available in the *Ridiculous Design Rules* series are *Never Use White Type on a Black Background and 50 other Ridiculous Design Rules* and *Never Leave the House Naked and 50 other Ridiculous Fashion Rules*.

Visit www.ridiculousdesignrules.com for more info.

The medium is the message

rule 01

The phrase 'the medium is the message' was coined back in 1964 by Canadian communication theorist Marshall McLuhan (1911–1980) in the book *Understanding Media: The Extensions of Man*. Just three years later McLuhan used the sentence again in a new book titled *The Medium is the Massage: An Inventory of Effects*. Upon seeing the typo in the book's title McLuhan allegedly exclaimed: "Leave it alone! It's great, and right on target!"

"In a culture like ours, long accustomed to splitting and dividing all things as a means of control, it is sometimes a bit of a shock to be reminded that, in operational and practical fact, the medium is the message. This is merely to say that the personal and social consequences of any medium – that is, of any extension of ourselves – result from the new scale that is introduced into our affairs by each extension of ourselves, or by any new technology."
Marshall McLuhan (1911–1980),
Canadian communication theorist

"The medium is the message. This is an overall rule of thumb for baby boomers. Boomers also tend to confuse emotions for thoughts, sentimentality for sensitivity and public relations for public policy."
Brad Holland (1943), American illustrator

"When it comes to advertising, should the medium or the message be decided first? The only fervent McLuhanites are we media planners, believing fervently that the medium can be the message. There are few ad people who wouldn't at least accept that the context in which a message is delivered can change consumers' perception of it."
Tess Alps (1953), British TV marketing executive

"Media don't have their own character any more. They used to; books and print had different, specific characteristics from TV and radio. Now many different media are concealed in, for example, the Internet medium. It's the software that makes the difference. It's more 'the method is the message'."
Mieke Gerritzen (1962), Dutch designer and director Graphic Design Museum

"I saw the political angle for Obey Giant as 'the medium is the message'. When something is illegally placed in the public right-of-way the very act itself makes it political. My hope was that in questioning what Obey Giant was about, the viewer would then begin to question all the images they were confronted with."
Shepard Fairey (1970), American artist, illustrator and graphic designer

"In graphic design there is usually a defined medium or message, and it's the designer's role to push and challenge the restrictions to create something that communicates."
Daniel Eatock (1975), British designer

Repetition, Repetition, Repetition

You want your message to stick. Chances of that happening are greatly increased by repeating the message. Again. And again. And again.

"Ads seem to work on the very advanced principle that a small pellet or pattern in a noisy, redundant barrage of repetition will gradually assert itself. Ads push the principle of noise all the way to the plateau of persuasion."
Marshall McLuhan (1911–1980), Canadian communication theorist

"Coke should return to the essence of their brand, which is the Real Thing. That's what is in people's minds. What are the three rules of advertising? Repetition, repetition, repetition. Use what's already in the minds of the consumers, which is they want to drink the real thing and not an imitation."
Al Ries (1926), American marketing expert

"The power of ads rests more in the repetition of obvious exhortations than in the subtle transmission of values."
Michael Schudson (1946), American sociologist

"About the only difference between the repetitious ads of the 20th century and the current crop is that the former were almost always loud, strident and didactic, resembling lessons taught to slow children. There was a lot of spelling out of brand names, one letter at a time,

and slogans reiterated perhaps a dozen times in 60 seconds. All that is pretty much gone; the irritant now is the constant frequency of the commercial rather than the fact the content is also annoying or obnoxious."
Stuart Elliott (1952), American advertising columnist of The New York Times

"Radio advertisement really hasn't changed that much. It's a great vehicle for local marketers. You can just sort of establish yourself as a local presence on the radio. You can go in and advertise a lot and repeat your message a lot… The thing about radio is that you don't need to be paying full attention. It just kind of gets in your brain, it kind of works its way in there through repetition."
Warren Berger (1958), American writer and journalist

"How do you become one of those brands that people want to wear on a T-shirt? There's no one commercial that's going to make me want to wear an Apple or a Nike T-shirt. It's a succession of many different impressions and moments. That's how marketing works now."
Jeff Hicks (1965), American advertising executive

Failure is always an option

Hate to break it to you, but not all campaigns will hit home. Failure is always an option. And all you can then do is pick yourself up. Dust yourself off. And fail all over again.

———————

"It used to be that a fellow went on the police force when everything else failed, but today he goes in the advertising game."
Frank McKinney Hubbard (1868-1930), American cartoonist and journalist

"To swear off making mistakes is very easy. All you have to do is swear off having ideas."
Leo Burnett (1891-1971), American advertising executive

"Ever tried? Ever failed? No matter. Try Again. Fail again. Fail better."
Samuel Beckett (1906-1989), Irish writer and playwright

"No, sir, I'm not saying that charming, witty and warm copy won't sell. I'm just saying I've seen thousands of charming, witty campaigns that didn't sell."
Rosser Reeves (1910-1984), American advertising executive

"It is important to admit your mistakes, and to do so before you are charged with them. Many clients are surrounded by buckpassers who make a fine art of blaming the agency for their own failures. I seize the earliest opportunity to assume the blame."
David Ogilvy (1911-1999), British advertising executive

for someone who makes a lot of mistakes

"I've worked with a couple of geniuses in my life. I've spent long hours making up for not being a genius. Nothing I do ever turns out exactly right. It's never what I expected."
Helmut Krone (1925-1996), American art director

"The secret of my success is failure and uncertainty."
Dan Wieden (1945), American advertising executive

"Enjoy failure and learn from it. You can never learn from success."
James Dyson (1947), British industrial designer

"Competence is the enemy. People who are competent are afraid to fail, afraid to experiment. They like being competent and defend it."
Seth Godin (1960), American marketing expert

DO YOUR RESEARCH

From focus groups to test panels and from trend analysis to consumer research. Just do it.

———

"Almost any question can be answered, cheaply, quickly and finally, by a test campaign. And that's the way to answer them – not by arguments around a table. Go to the court of last resort – the buyers of your product."
Claude C. Hopkins (1866-1932), American advertising pioneer

"The most important word in the vocabulary of advertising is TEST. If you pretest your product with consumers, and pretest your advertising, you will do well in the marketplace."
David Ogilvy (1911-1999), British advertising executive

"We don't ask research to do what it was never meant to do, and that is to get an idea."
Bill Bernbach (1911-1982), American advertising executive

"Great ideas can't be tested. Only mediocre ideas can be tested."
George Lois (1931), American advertising executive

"We tend to believe that people lie in focus groups because they're trying to impress the rest of the people sitting around the table eating the M&Ms."
Chuck Porter (1945), American advertising executive

"I hate to tell you, but I'm not a big believer in market research either. I believe you take your inspiration and throw it out there. If it sticks, praise God. If it doesn't, you can listen to research and try to fix, and then you throw it out there again. But I don't believe a focus group has ever created a revolution."
Guy Kawasaki (1954), marketing guru

"It's really hard to design products by focus groups. A lot of times, people don't know what they want until you show it to them."
Steve Jobs (1955), co-founder of Apple and Pixar

"This business has been founded on consumer research, trend analysis, and focus groups, so that advertisers can find a way to piggyback on a trend."
Jeff Hicks (1965), American advertising executive

"Asked about the power of advertising in research surveys, most agree that it works, but not on them."
Eric Clark, British journalist and author

"[I'm not a] fan of using market research to predict future behavior. Consumers are just not able to tell you what they are likely to do in the future… Research should be used to understand the current mind of the consumer. What your brand and your competitors brand stand for in the mind. Research is helpful to find out what consumers did and what they think about a particular brand."
Laura Ries (1971), American marketing expert

Follow the money

Dan Wieden (1945), American advertising executive and co-founder of Wieden+Kennedy said it best: "In this business, you follow one of two masters: you either follow the muse or you follow the dollar..."

"Two common conceptions with regard to advertising which are held by a considerable number of people are that enormously large sums of money are expended for it, and that much of this expenditure is an economic waste."
Daniel Starch (1883-1979), American advertising executive

"Advertising is, actually, a simple phenomenon in terms of economics. It is merely a substitute for a personal sales force – an extension, if you will, of the merchant who cries aloud his wares."
Rosser Reeves (1910-1984), American advertising executive

"Expensive advertising courts us with hints and images. The ordinary kind merely says, Buy."
Mason Cooley (1927-2002), American aphorist

"Advertising is totally unnecessary. Unless you hope to make money."
Jef I. Richards (1955), American advertising professor

"Small brands with modest media budgets can end up having greater cultural impact than the big spenders – if they're willing and able to come at the audience with something that has never been seen before."
Warren Berger (1958), American writer and journalist

"A tight budget is the mother of invention. If they don't have any money, that means that they need me a lot."
Andrew Keller (1970), American advertising executive

"A lot of the focus on advertising is really a matter of people just following the money."
Alex Bogusky (1963), American advertising executive

MAKE IT MEMORABLE

rule
06

You want your slogan, logo or ad to make a lasting impression. Making it memorable is the goal. Humor, shock tactics and massive exposure are just some of the means.

"Make it simple. Make it memorable. Make it inviting to look at. Make it fun to read."
Leo Burnett (1891-1971), American advertising executive

"The headline is the most important element of an ad. It must offer a promise to the reader of a believable benefit. And it must be phrased in a way to make it memorable."
Morris Hite (1910-1983), American businessman

"Nobody counts the number of ads you run: they just remember the impression you make."
Bill Bernbach (1911-1982), American advertising executive

"How easily is the brand element re-called? How easily recognized? Is this true at both purchase and consumption? Short brand names such as Tide, Crest, and Puffs can help."
Philip Kotler (1931), American International Marketing professor, and Kevin Lane Keller (1950), American Marketing professor

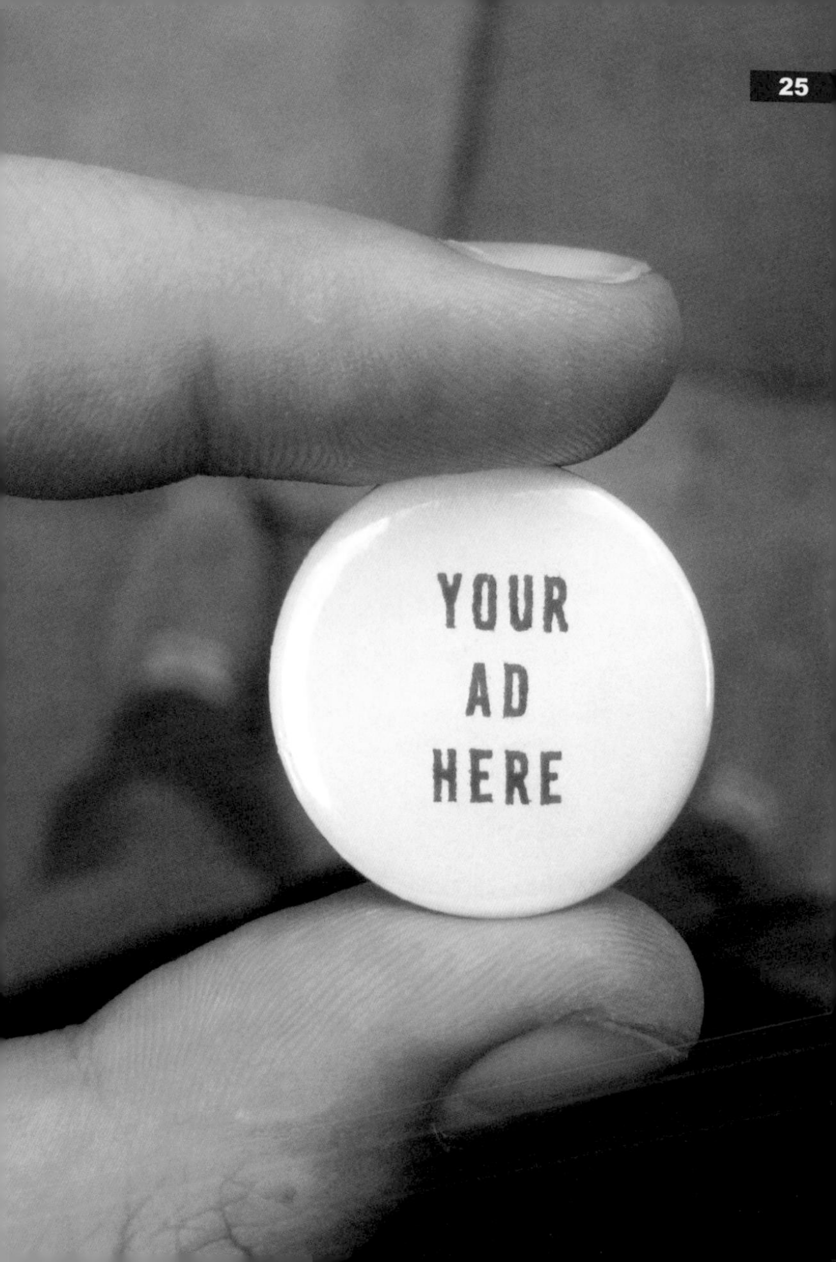
YOUR
AD
HERE

Advertising is evil

rule 07

Advertising evil? Well, not according to Mr. Advertising David Ogilvy, who argued that "advertising is only evil when it advertises evil things."

"I can not think of any circumstances in which advertising would not be an evil."
Arnold Toynbee (1889-1975), British historian

"[History will see advertising] as one of the real evil things of our time. It is stimulating people constantly to want things, want this, want that."
Malcolm Muggeridge (1903-1990), British journalist

"Why, I ask, isn't it possible that advertising as a whole is a fantastic fraud, presenting an image of America taken seriously by no one, least of all by the advertising men who create it?"
David Riesman (1909-2002) American sociologist

"Political advertising ought to be stopped. It's the only really dishonest kind of advertising that's left. It's totally dishonest."
David Ogilvy (1911-1999), British advertising executive

"It is flagrantly dishonest for an advertising agent to urge consumers to buy a product which he would not allow his own wife to buy."
David Ogilvy (1911-1999), British advertising executive

"Young people are threatened... by the evil use of advertising techniques that stimulate the natural inclination to avoid hard work by promising the immediate satisfaction of every desire."

Pope John Paul II (1920- 2005)

"Certainly, it seems true enough that there's a good deal of irony in the world... I mean, if you live in a world full of politicians and advertising, there's obviously a lot of deception."
Kenneth Koch (1925-2002), American poet and playwright

"Advertising men and politicians are dangerous if they are separated. Together they are diabolical."
Phillip Adams (1939), Australian writer, producer and broadcaster

"Mass consumption, advertising, and mass art are a corporate Frankenstein; while they reinforce the system, they also undermine it."
Ellen Willis (1941- 2006), American political essayist and journalist

"If it's not done ethically, advertising won't be trusted. If consumers don't trust it, advertising is pointless."
Jef I. Richards (1955), American advertising professor

"I don't think there is anything wrong with logos, with doing whatever is necessary to get your message out. Among some of the people who share my ideas, there's an attitude that the act of selling is somehow dirty. But I think that if you're actually selling what you're claiming to sell, then it's fine. I have a problem when there is a betrayal in the message."
Naomi Klein (1970), Canadian journalist and author

erism

Make it pretty

French-born American industrial designer Raymond Loewy (1893-1986) summed it up perfectly: "Ugliness does not sell."

"I regard a great ad as the most beautiful thing in the world."
Leo Burnett (1891-1971), American advertising executive

"Great designers seldom make great advertising men, because they get overcome by the beauty of the picture – and forget that merchandise must be sold."
James Randolph Adams (1898-1956), American advertising executive

"Without aesthetic, design is either the humdrum repetition of familiar clichés or a wild scramble for novelty. Without the aesthetic, the computer is but a mindless speed machine, producing effects without substance. Form without relevant content, or content without meaningful form."
Paul Rand (1914-1996), American graphic designer

"When did Marketing become the make-it-pretty department?"
Sylvia Reynolds, American marketing officer Wells Fargo

"Make it like a sunflower."
Steve Jobs (1955), co-founder of Apple and Pixar

"The best ad is a good product."

American advertising executive Alan H. Meyer was on to something when he said that the best ad is a good product, although in all fairness, a good ad never hurt anybody.

———

"If advertisers spent the same amount of money on improving their products as they do on advertising then they wouldn't have to advertise them."
Will Rogers (1879-1935), American humorist

"The product that will not sell without advertising will not sell profitably with advertising."
Albert Lasker (1880-1952), American businessman

"You must make the product interesting, not just make the ad different. And that's what too many of the copywriters in the U.S. today don't yet understand."
Rosser Reeves (1910-1984), American advertising executive

"Advertising doesn't create a product advantage. It can only convey it."
Bill Bernbach (1911-1982), American advertising executive

"I always use my clients' products. This is not toadyism, but elementary good manners."
David Ogilvy (1911-1999), British advertising executive

"There is a great deal of advertising that is much better than the product. When that happens, all that the good advertising will do is put you out of business faster."
Jerry Della Famina (1936), American advertising executive

"The only way to advertise is by not focusing on the product."
Calvin Klein (1942), American fashion designer

"A great product can market itself if it's designed to do so."
Alex Bogusky (1963), American advertising executive

"The future of advertising is great products that have marketing embedded in them."
Jeff Hicks (1965), American advertising executive

"For me, the product is very much at the center of the experience. It's very much at the center of what you want to communicate or what you're about. I think no matter what business you're in, the right way to do it is to conceive your message, the idea of what you're about, at the same time as you are making the actual product. I always find myself pushing for an earlier involvement in the process from agencies."
Yves Béhar (1967), Swiss-born industrial designer

One Plus One Equals Three

German-born American artist Josef Albers (1888-1976) argued that "in design sometimes one plus one equals three," the implication being that sometimes the end product is greater than the sum of its parts. Like when two brands come together to create a (temporary) super brand.

"Everything I did was looking for the Big Idea, but you're not going to get to an idea thinking visually in most cases. You have to think in words, then add the visual. Then you can make one plus one equal three."
George Lois (1931), American advertising executive

"Where you really get the 'one plus one equals three' is to include viral into the mix of media. Involving traditional media is an important step."
Jeff Hicks (1965), American advertising executive

"Co-branding might sound simple, but the wedding of successful brands doesn't necessarily guarantee that the partnership will grow as a successful marriage... Half of the world's marriages break down, and all but 10 percent of brands fail to maintain their co-branding partnerships. So, without any doubt, there's space for substantial improvement. And, needless to say, you'll see substantial savings in your marketing budget if you marry the right brand the first time."
Martin Lindstrom (1970), Danish brand expert

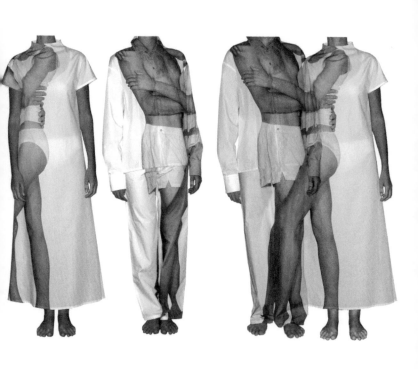

Advertising is a guessing game

You can tick all the right boxes, hire the best art directors, get a great jingle, an even better slogan and one heck of a viral campaign and still end up with a failure, proving that you can lead a horse to water, but you can't make it drink.

———

"The fact is that most marketing, advertising, and branding strategies are a guessing game – and those ads that happen to meet success are considered in hindsight, pure kismet. Until now, marketers and advertisers haven't really known what drives our behavior, so they've had to rely on luck, coincidence, chance or repeating the same old tricks all over again."
Martin Lindstrom (1970), Danish brand expert

"You can take a scientific approach when designing campaigns and map everything out but then you end up with everybody doing the same kind of campaigns... but I think it's important to keep in mind that ads can be art as well. Of course you can run an ad by a test group and see how people respond but sometimes you also need to rely on your own intuition."
Chris Barrett, British advertising executive

"Word of mouth is the best medium of all."

rule 12

Word of mouth is the best medium of all. But don't take my word for it, as it was actually American advertising guru Bill Bernbach (1911-1982) who first said it: "You cannot sell a man who isn't listening; word of mouth is the best medium of all; and dullness won't sell your product, but neither will irrelevant brilliance."

"While it may be true that the best advertising is word-of-mouth, never lose sight of the fact it also can be the worst advertising."
Jef I. Richards (1955), American advertising professor

"Word of mouth is great, except when it isn't."
Bob Garfield (1955), American ad critic and journalist

"The beauty of interactive websites is that they can engage people longer and more deeply than a commercial ever could – at a fraction of the cost. The best sites tend to get passed along from one person to another, creating the kind of grass-roots, word-of-mouth promotion that's worth its weight in gold."
Warren Berger (1958), American writer and journalist

"The lesson to take away is that since Christians are the most socially connected demographic in the country (most meet face to face at least twice per week) you must give them the tools to spread the word about your film, product, or service."
Bob Hutchins (1965), American faith-based marketing specialist

"There's the rise of word-of-mouth influence on marketing communications. It's really something quite significant for the whole industry. How do you fuel positive word of mouth? You have to be more inventive, come up with more imaginative strategies. Studying leading-edge cultures can give you inspiration, ways of targeting key people for fueling word of mouth: the tastemakers, the influential people."
Zoe Lazarus (1970), British trend analyst

"Discovery is now a big part of marketing. If you find out about something that's not in the mainstream, you like to disseminate the information yourself, because it gives you kudos with your peer group, whether on the golf course or in the schoolyard."
Richard Welch (1973), British trend analyst

"People engage in word of mouth because they want to look good. Word of mouth is the most honest advertising medium there is. People don't want to hurt their friends and family and colleagues with bad information."
George Silverman, author of The Secrets of Word-of-Mouth Marketing *(2001)*

KEEP
CALM
AND
rule
13
MAKE
THE LOGO
BIGGER

It may sound crude but in the world of advertising sex sells and size matters.

"Most corporations think the logo is a kind of rabbit's foot or talisman – although sometimes it can be an albatross – and believe that if it is altered, something terrible will happen."
Paul Rand (1914-1996), American graphic designer

"Logos are dead. Long live icons and avatars."
Marty Neumeier (1947), American communication designer, writer and publisher

"I was once asked by a client to create a logo that would win an Addy Award. Luckily, I have a drawerful of pencils for just such an occasion."
Rodney Davidson (1957), American graphic designer

"A logo should look just as good in 15-foot letters on top of company headquarters as it does one sixteenth of an inch tall on company stationery."
Steven Gilliatt, American brand specialist

"I've yet to have a client ask me to make them look smaller than they are."
Bill Gardner (1957), American graphic designer

"Clients are about their logos like guys are about their... you know. They love talking about them. They love to look at them. They want you to look at them. They think the bigger they are, the more effective they are. And they try to sneak looks at other guys' logos when they can. But as any woman will tell you, nobody cares."
Luke Sullivan, author of Hey, Whipple, Squeeze This: A Guide to Creating Great Ads *(2008)*

Advertising is storytelling

Where does storytelling end and lying begin? Is there even a line dividing the two? Or is it just the same product with a different label?

———

"When you don't have a story to tell, it is often a good thing to make your package the subject of your illustration."
David Ogilvy (1911-1999), British advertising executive

"I'm not sure television is where the most revolutionary work is taking place right now. Production budgets have shrunk, which should not be a brake on creativity, but there's not as much psychic energy in television as there is in the interactive space. But it's still an incredibly magic medium that has the ability to engage you emotionally in ways that few other mediums do. It's great for storytelling."
Dan Wieden (1945), American advertising executive

"I think that while markets are conversations, marketing is a story. Starbucks creates conversations among customers, so does Apple. The NYSE makes a fortune permitting people to interact with each other. But great marketing is storytelling, and if you've been to a Broadway show lately, you'll notice that audience participation is discouraged. That doesn't mean that great playwrights don't listen! They do. They, like great marketers, listen relentlessly. They engage in offline conversations constantly. They poll and they do censuses and most important, they have true conversations with small groups of real people. But THEN, they tell a story."

Seth Godin (1960), American marketing expert

SHE SAID h

ONE WAY

...E TO **STOP** SLEEPING TOGETHER AND WALKED OUT OF THE ROOM. ...O I INFLATED THE AEROBED, HOPING TO ...PTURE THE AIR THAT BREATHED THOSE WORDS. THEN LAY DOWN, AND GROUND MY PELVIS INTO IT.

THERE'S A PLACE WHERE

HERE

aerobed® *NOW WHO'S ON TOP?*

There is no such thing as bad publicity

rule
15

As the old Hollywood adage will have it there really is no such thing as bad publicity.

"I would rather be attacked than unnoticed."
Samuel Johnson (1709-1784), British author

"Publicity, publicity, publicity is the greatest moral factor and force in our public life."
Joseph Pulitzer (1847-1911), Hungarian-American publisher

"There is no such thing as bad publicity except your own obituary."
Brendan Behan (1923-1964), Irish author and dramatist

"There is such a thing as bad publicity."
Joyce Brothers (1927), American psychologist

"Good publicity is preferable to bad, but from the bottom line perspective bad publicity is better than none. Bad publicity is sometimes better than no publicity at all."
Donald Trump (1946), American businessman

Product placement doesn't work

Fast food chains, car companies, watch makers and sunglasses manufacturers happily pay big bucks to be featured in Hollywood blockbusters and computer games. Never mind the fact that the effect of this blatant form of advertising is yet to be proven.

"Bullshit. Total fucking bullshit."
David Lynch (1946), American director on product placement

"Before product placement became a lucrative business, movie studios mostly kept well-known brands off the screen. They generally considered the appearance of real products to be too great a distraction from the escapist worlds they conjured up for moviegoers at neighborhood cinemas."
Stuart Elliott (1952), American advertising columnist of The New York Times

"The value of product placement is unproven but even if it was half as effective as spot ads the number of genuine opportunities that could exist per hour of broadcasting will be tiny."
Tess Alps (1953), British TV marketing executive

"The vast majority of sponsorship and product placement doesn't work because it is aimed at the conscious part of the brain, which neuroscience tells us accounts for no more than 15 per cent of our cognitive capacity."
Martin Lindstrom (1970), Danish brand expert

"The ultimate form of product placement is in our minds, when brand names stand in for everyday nouns and verbs."
Alex Frankel (1970), American writer and brand observer

Get them while they're young

Lifelong customer loyalty: it's the Holy Grail of advertising. And just as difficult to obtain. But that certainly doesn't stop brands and marketers from targeting the underage consumer.

———

"If advertising has invaded the judgment of children, it has also forced its way into the family, an insolent usurper of parental function, degrading parents to mere intermediaries between their children and the market."
Jules Henry (1904-1969), American anthropologist

"How many new parents clutch their baby to their breast and declare, 'I want this child to grow up to be a media planner'?"

Jef I. Richards (1955), American advertising professor

"Younger people create the trends that are aped by the rest of us. The brands young people choose, niche and marginal at first, become, by definition, cool and desirable. Over-50s may well have more money, but they are deeply influenced by the brands young people buy. That's because we are all still 25 in our heads, and particularly so for products that have nothing to do with the practical physical needs of older people. So it makes sense to pursue the trendsetters and opinion-formers and let the rest of us follow."
Tess Alps (1953), British TV marketing executive

"There are a lot of players in the youth or alternative marketing space. It's a tough jungle out there. Plenty of companies will give it the old college try and just end up as part of the noise."
Samantha Skey (1972), American youth marketing expert

HOPE SELLS

Hope sells. Or better yet, advertising sells hope.

"The philosophy behind much advertising is based on the old observation that every man is really two men – the man he is and the man he wants to be."
William A. Feather (1889-1981), American author and publisher

"The work of an advertising agency is warmly and immediately human. It deals with human needs, wants, dreams and hopes. Its 'product' cannot be turned out on an assembly line."
Leo Burnett (1891-1971), American advertising executive

"We grew up founding our dreams on the infinite promise of American advertising. I still believe that one can learn to play the piano by mail and that mud will give you a perfect complexion."
Zelda Fitzgerald (1900-1948), American author

"In our factory, we make lipstick. In our advertising, we sell hope."
Charles Revson (1906-1975), Canadian businessman of Revlon fame

"Hope for the best. Expect the worst. Life is a play. We're unrehearsed"
Mel Brooks (1926), American film director, comedian and actor

"Hope in the face of difficulty. Hope in the face of uncertainty. The audacity of hope! In the end, that is God's greatest gift to us, the bedrock of this nation. A belief in things not seen. A belief that there are better days ahead."
Barack Obama (1961), 44th American President

"If the superfan culture that brought Obama to power is going to transform itself into an independent political movement, one fierce enough to produce programs capable of meeting the current crises, we are all going to have to stop hoping and start demanding."
Naomi Klein (1970), Canadian journalist and author

Accentuate the positive

It's like Bing 'The Crooner' Crosby (1903-1977) used to sing: "You've got to accentuate the positive. Eliminate the negative. Latch on to the affirmative. Don't mess with Mister In-Between."

"Delete the negative: accentuate the positive!"
Donna Karan (1948), American fashion designer

"It seems counterintuitive to accentuate the positive amid all the downbeat financial news. But Madison Avenue is typically a place called Hope. Besides, gloom-mongering could convince consumers to put off what little spending they still intend."
Stuart Elliott (1952), American advertising columnist of The New York Times

"Try to find that long-neglected truth in a product and give it a hug."
Alex Bogusky (1963), American advertising executive

Eliminate the negative

rule
20

Have an idea

A bit of a no-brainer, but it all starts with an idea. That little light bulb moment that sparks creativity and that gets the juices flowing.

"To get your ideas across, use small words, big ideas and short sentences."
John Henry Patterson (1844-1922), American businessman

"Creative ideas flourish best in a shop which preserves some spirit of fun. Nobody is in business for fun, but that does not mean there cannot be fun in business."
Leo Burnett (1891-1971), American advertising executive

"If an ad campaign is built around a weak idea – or as is so often the case, no idea at all – I don't give a damn how good the execution is, it's going to fail."
Morris Hite (1910-1983), American businessman

"An idea can turn to dust or magic, depending on the talent that rubs against it."
Bill Bernbach (1911-1982), American advertising executive

"Big ideas are so hard to recognize, so fragile, so easy to kill. Don't forget that, all of you who don't have them."
John Elliott Jr. (1921-2005), American advertising executive

"Great ideas, not channels, create buzz."
Jeff Hicks (1965), American advertising executive

"It doesn't matter what medium a great idea lives in. So when we're initially thinking about campaigns, we aren't really thinking about TV scripts or print ads. It's about generating great ideas. We find the medium they live in later."
Jeff Benjamin (1975), American advertising executive

"You have to have the passion, confidence, and work ethic to believe you can continue to come up with more good ideas, if and when your original 'good' idea gets bludgeoned to death."
Alex Bogusky (1963), American advertising executive

Never use pop-up ads

If you think that the average surfer only hates pop-up ads, think again. In June 2009, Nicholas Carlson, editor at Silicon Alley Insider, published an impressive list of 'online ad formats people hate most', based on a survey carried out by usability testing firm Catalyst Group. Turns out that besides the old pop-up ad, people also hate:

- Banner ads below headers
- Ads that look like content
- Dancing ads
- Auto-expanding half-page ads
- Banners next to logos
- Billboards in the top right corner
- Google text links interrupting content
- Ads with hidden close buttons
- Interstitials
- Page Take-overs

"I can't understand the nerve of some Web users who complain about seeing a pop-up ad on our site. I give you a photo of a beautiful woman, and you bitch and moan about a stupid pop-up window? Give me a break!"
Gerard van der Leun (1945),
Penthouse.com director

"Internet advertising will rapidly lose its value and its impact, for reasons that can easily be understood. Traditional advertising simply cannot be carried over to the internet, replacing full-page ads on the back of The New York Times or 30-second spots on the Super Bowl broadcast with pop-ups, banners, click-throughs on side bars. … Online advertising cannot deliver all that is asked of it. It is going to be smaller, not larger, than it is today. It cannot support all the applications and all the content we want on the internet."
Eric K. Clemons (1948), American Professor of Operations and Information Management

"I haven't spoken to any people who say 'I love pop-ups, send me more of them', but they are part of a quid pro quo. If you want to enjoy the content of a website that is free, the pop-ups come with it."
David J. Moore (1952), American online advertising executive

"If we target the right ad to the right person at the right time and they click it, we win."
Eric E. Schmidt (1955), American chief executive Google

Jeg ser ✕

[...]

Jeg ser, jeg ser . . .
Jeg er vist kommet på en feil klode!
Her er så underligt . . .

OK

Sex sells

Sex sells. And so on a daily basis we're bombarded with semi-naked bodies, sweaty six-packs and sexually-explicit taglines that are used to push anything from soft drinks to shower gel.

———

"If we define pornography as any message from any communication medium that is intended to arouse sexual excitement, then it is clear that most advertisements are covertly pornographic."
Philip Slater (1927), American sociologist, author and playwright

"Society drives people crazy with lust and calls it advertising."
John Lahr (1941), American theater critic

"I'm a sexual person, and that's reflected in my clothes and my advertisements."
Calvin Klein (1942), American fashion designer

"So sex certainly sells media products, and it can work for others, where permitted. Advertising, quite rightly, is not allowed the same latitude as editorial, because it arrives unsolicited and unannounced. However, advertising needs to keep up with shifts in consumer attitudes, or it risks looking quaint and irrelevant."
Tess Alps (1953), British TV marketing executive

"In advertising, sex sells. But only if you're selling sex."
Jef I. Richards (1955), American advertising professor

"Sex doesn't sell, controversy does."
Martin Lindstrom (1970), Danish brand expert

DON'T Believe THE HYPE!

Whether or not most advertising is indeed hype is besides the point, the mere fact that there are consumers out there who believe this to be true should be enough to make many a marketer more than a little nervous about using 'new and improved' and other cliché slogans.

"Today, 3,000 marketing messages a day flow into the average North American brain. That's more hype, clutter, sex and violence than many of us can handle on top of all the other pressures of modern life."
Kalle Lasn (1942), Estonian-born publisher Adbusters magazine

"This notion that hype might somehow be shaped into a practical and useful form is not a new one: it goes way back, at least to the 1890s, when an ambitious printer named Henry Beach started changing companies to have their names printed on the handles of flyswatters – one of the first great practical pieces of what has come to be known through the years as 'swag'."
Warren Berger (1958), American writer and journalist

"In a world of hype, a few candid words can be more powerful than a thousand empty slogans and claims."
Warren Berger (1958), American writer and journalist

"In order to have people talk about you and your ideas, you must resist the urge to hype your products and services."
David Meerman Scott (1961), American marketing strategist

"At worst, advertising is seen as hype, unfair capitalistic manipulation, banal commercial noise, mind control, postmodern voodoo, or outright deception. At best, the average person sees advertising as amusing, informative, helpful, and occasionally hip. The truth about advertising lies somewhere between the extremes."
Thomas O'Guinn, Chris Allen, and Richard J. Semenik in Advertising and Integrated Brand Promotion *(2008)*

"People do not believe the advertising hype because they know better. They are too smart."
Lynn Thorne in Word of Mouth Advertising Online & Off *(2008)*

Advertising is a business of words

Ogilvy called advertising a business of words, but also noted that unfortunately advertising agencies are crawling with men and women who can't write: "They cannot write advertisements, and they cannot write plans. They are as helpless as deaf mutes on the stage of the Metropolitan Opera."

———————

"The simplest definition of advertising, and one that will probably meet the test of critical examination, is that advertising is selling in print."
Daniel Starch (1883-1979), American advertising executive

"I have learned that it is far easier to write a speech about good advertising than it is to write a good ad."
Leo Burnett (1891-1971), American advertising executive

"The trouble with us in America isn't that the poetry of life has turned to prose, but that it has turned to advertising copy."
Louis Kronenberger (1904-1980), American critic

"Writing advertising copy is like playing chess with yourself, or solo scrabble. In any case, I preferred it to having to ask for a grant."
Cees Nooteboom (1933), Dutch author

"As advertising blather becomes the nation's normal idiom, language becomes printed noise."
George Will (1941), American journalist

"Advertising is speech. It's regulated because it's often effective speech."
Jef I. Richards (1955), American advertising professor

WORDSAR
ENTALWAY
SMEANTT
OBEREAD

Sell them what they want, not what they need

rule 26

The advertising industry as a whole has but one aim and that is to create desire. The object is to make people want things that they might already have or don't really need. Now, who said advertising isn't an art?

"I do not read advertisements – I would spend all my time wanting things."
Franz Kafka (1883-1924), Czech writer

"Advertising says to people, 'Here's what we've got. Here's what it will do for you. Here's how to get it'."
Leo Burnett (1891-1971), American advertising executive

"Good advertising does not just circulate information. It penetrates the public mind with desires and belief."
Leo Burnett (1891-1971), American advertising executive

"Advertising degrades the people it appeals to: it deprives them of their will to choose."
Carrie P. Snow (1905-1980), British novelist and scientist

"It is not the purpose of the ad or commercial to make the reader or listener say, 'My what a clever ad'. It is the purpose of advertising to make the reader say, 'I believe I'll buy one when I'm shopping tomorrow'."

Morris Hite (1910-1983), American businessman

"We read advertisements... to discover and enlarge our desires. We are always ready – even eager – to discover, from the announcement of a new product, what we have all along wanted without really knowing it."
Daniel J. Boorstin (1914-2004), American historian

"Advertising is found in societies which have passed the point of satisfying the basic animal needs."
Marion Harper Jr. (1916-1989), American advertising executive

"Consider the sheer superfluity of certain kinds of goods which this forcing of turnover entails. We are deluged with things which we do not wear, which we lose, which go out of style, which make unwelcome presents for our friends, which disappear anyhow… Here the advertiser plays on the essential monkey within us, and uses up mountains of good iron ore and countless sturdy horse power to fill – a few months later – the wagon of the junk man."
Stuart Chase and Frederick John Schlink, American authors of Your Money's Worth: A Study in the Waste of the Consumer's Dollar (1927)

"The best advertising should make you nervous about what you're not buying."
Mary Wells Lawrence (1928), American advertising executive

"We are hunter-gatherers, sure. I still enjoy getting something, bringing it home and showing it to my wife. When her face lights up that satisfies me. So our genes are hard-wired. But there is also the environment. Since the second world war we have created a consumer culture pumping something like 3,000 to 5,000 messages into our brains every day from the time you are a baby, when you count logos on products. I don't think we're wired to deal with this curveball that is coming. This whole human experiment of ours on planet Earth is now in big trouble, and here we are sipping our lattes and listening to good music in our S.U.V.s."
Kalle Lasn (1942), Estonian-born publisher Adbusters magazine

"People do not know what they want until a brilliant person shows them."
Maurice Saatchi (1946), Iraqi-born British advertising executive

ACQUA DI
GIÒ
GIORGIO ARMANI

HAVE FUN

rule
27

Sticking to creative briefs and meeting sales figures is fine, but don't forget to have some fun along the way.

"Fun without sell gets nowhere but sell without fun tends to become obnoxious."
Leo Burnett (1891-1971), American advertising executive

"In my opinion, fun is what makes advertising successful."
Leo Bogart (1921-2005), American sociologist and marketing expert

"Advertising is the most fun you can have with your clothes on."
Jerry Della Femina (1936), American advertising executive

"The fun image that advertising has traditionally enjoyed is now giving way to a much darker picture of advertising as mental pollution."
Kalle Lasn (1942), Estonian-born publisher Adbusters magazine

"The ad industry isn't struggling for a new set of principles or abandoning the ones that made it great from the start. It's simply in the midst of a business cycle. I don't think it's more profound than that. And despite the economic downturn, I'm having more fun today than at any other moment in my 30-year advertising career."
Shelly Lazarus (1947), American advertising executive

"What PR people need to realize is that nobody cares about your products (except you). What people do care about are themselves and ways to solve their problems. People also like to be entertained and to share in something remarkable."
David Meerman Scott (1961), American marketing strategist

STICK TO THE BILLBOARD BASICS

- LOCATION, LOCATION, LOCATION
- ALWAYS INCLUDE A LOGO
- BUY IN BULK (1 BILLBOARD DOES NOT MAKE A CAMPAIGN)
- USE 7 WORDS, OR LESS

Outdoor advertising is considered by some to be marketing's magic bullet but in a public domain that is covered with slogans, huge billboards and neon signs you have to stick to some basic billboard rules if you don't want to see your campaign backfire.

———

"The Municipal Art Society of New York and the National Highways Association's Division of Municipal Art are co-operating in a campaign against the disfigurement of the streets, the architecture, the parkways, the vistas of the City of New York by the overgrown and ever-growing, universal, all-defacing billboard."
The Billboard Evil *article, as published in The New York Times in 1916*

"We are bombarded with thousands of direct marketing messages a day, very few of which we are able to take in, let alone process into changing buying behavior. Having a logo on the perimeter board is not worth the money, there has to be a synergy, where the brand becomes synonymous with the sport, and better still, becomes a ritual."
Martin Lindstrom (1970), Danish brand expert

"It's about moderation. The city can sometimes overload its public spaces with huge advertisements (which give the most revenue) and at the same time cut down on the more personal advertisements (which give no revenue). This contradictory stance needs balance."
Dave Bell (1970), Scottish advertising executive KesselsKramer

"In an ideal world, advertising is a fully integrated part of a city's architecture and is respectful of the surroundings in which it operates."
Tom Himpe (1976), Belgian-born strategic planner and author of Advertising is Dead, Long Live Advertising

"If you go to Times Square in New York or Piccadilly Circus in London, advertising is all over the place. You'll have a hard time finding a blank spot, where advertising has not intruded. The simple logic is this: where there are people, there is attention to be grabbed. And that's worth a lot of money. So that's an inevitable force. But there is also a balance to be found. In the end, it's in advertising's own best interest to be careful about not polluting the city too much. Because the more advertising there is, the less it gets noticed and the less impact it has."
Tom Himpe (1976), Belgian-born strategic planner and author of Advertising is Dead, Long Live Advertising

Bad advertising is better than no advertising at all

rule 29

This rather peculiar rule, which probably comes courtesy of one serious bad advertiser, puts the ridiculous in ridiculous advertising rules.

"I have learned that any fool can write a bad ad, but that it takes a real genius to keep his hands off a good one."
Leo Burnett (1891-1971), American advertising executive

"Doing business without advertising is like winking at a girl in the dark. You know what you are doing, but nobody else does."
Steuart Henderson Britt (1907-1979), American advertising consultant

"I know of a brewer who sells more of his beer to the people who never see his advertising than to the people who see it every week. Bad advertising can unsell a product."
David Ogilvy (1911-1999), British advertising executive

"Bad advertising can be harmful to your health. Maybe it should carry a health warning."
Sir Frank Lowe, British advertising executive

"There's so much truly putrid advertising out there it's embarrassing. But not all advertising is bad. Some of it is really quite mediocre."
Jef I. Richards (1955), American advertising professor

DETERMINE YOUR TARGET AUDIENCE

Before you can even think about making the hard or soft sell, you need to establish and get to know your target audience. It's like American advertising executive Leo Burnett once said: "If you can't turn yourself into your customer, you probably shouldn't be in the ad writing business at all."

"Anyone who thinks that people can be fooled or pushed around has an inaccurate and pretty low estimate of people – and he won't do very well in advertising."
Leo Burnett (1891-1971), American advertising executive

"If advertising had a little more respect for the public, the public would have a lot more respect for advertising."
James Randolph Adams (1898-1956), American advertising executive

"There is no such thing as a Mass Mind. The Mass Audience is made up of individuals, and good advertising is written always from one person to another. When it is aimed at millions it rarely moves anyone."
Fairfax Cone (1903-1977), American advertising executive

"There is no such thing as national advertising. All advertising is local and personal. It's one man or woman reading one newspaper in the kitchen or watching TV in the den."
Morris Hite (1910-1983), American businessman

"Even if it is true that the average man seems most comfortable with the commonplace and familiar, it is equally true that catering to bad taste, which we so readily attribute to the average reader, merely perpetuates that mediocrity and denies the reader one of the most easily accessible means for aesthetic development and eventual enjoyment."
Paul Rand (1914-1996), American graphic designer

"Marketing to a Christian audience is no different than any other audience – just that they exercise choice based on a value system. Once the faith-based community can get behind something and they believe in it, they will pass it along."
Bob Hutchins (1965), American faith-based marketing specialist

CLIENT

RIGHT

THE CLIENT IS ALWAYS RIGHT

The client might be king but there is a real difference between having to deal with a benevolent ruler or a cruel despot.

"When a customer enters my store, forget me. He is king."
John Wanamaker (1838-1922), American businessman

"I have learned that trying to guess what the boss or the client wants is the most debilitating of all influences in the creation of good advertising."
Leo Burnett (1891-1971), American advertising executive

"It takes good clients to make a good advertising agency. Regardless of how much talent an ad agency may have, it is ineffective without good products and services to advertise."
Morris Hite (1910-1983), American businessman

"I like things that are playful; I like things that are happy; I like things that will make the client smile."
Paul Rand (1914-1996), American graphic designer

"In advertising, I was frustrated by having to deal with the client. It was the only time I really worked in a proper office, and I didn't like it – simple as that."
Terry Gilliam (1940), American writer and filmmaker

"Being independent provides the freedom to do what you feel is right and that includes the freedom to tell a difficult client to screw off."
Dan Wieden (1945), American advertising executive

A good jingle does it every time

Ogilvy once stated that 'the advertisers who believe in the selling power of jingles have never had to sell anything'. Wise words, which dispel the myth that a good jingle does it every time. Having said that, a good ad campaign can launch a music career – just think back to the 250,000 bouncing balls that provided Swedish singer José 'Heartbeats' González with a worldwide hit.

—————

"If you went into a store and asked a salesman to show you a refrigerator, how would you react if he started singing at you? Yet some clients feel short-changed if you don't give them a jingle."
David Ogilvy (1911-1999), British advertising executive

"It is difficult to produce a television documentary that is both incisive and probing when every twelve minutes one is interrupted by twelve dancing rabbits singing about toilet paper."
Rod Serling (1924-1975), American producer and screenwriter

"The spots that we remember through the years are the ones that sang to us about a product, or danced for us about the product, or entertained us musically about the product for 30 seconds. Ask anyone over 30 what's in a Big Mac, and they will tell you… because it was sung."
Steve Karmen (1937), American jingle composer and producer

"Years ago you'd hear the same commercials over and over again and you'd hear the same slogans and jingles and it would sort of get drummed into your head. That doesn't happen so much on TV anymore because of the splintered television audience. But it still happens on radio. In radio you can still get in there and hit somebody 20 times a day with your message and believe me that really gets into their head."
Warren Berger (1958), American writer and journalist

"There was a period of time in America where the advertising world actually went to the housewives of America and had them write jingles that would appeal to them. It was actually brilliant marketing."
Julianne Moore (1960), American actress

"The jingle is dead."
Eric Korte, music director at Saatchi & Saatchi

"Once upon a time [selling a song to an advertiser] was a pact with the devil. Now totally legitimate artists are thrilled to perform mini-concerts for ad people. The whole paradigm has shifted. The labels have no money to promote music. They're the driving force behind this."
Gregory Grene (1965), American musician and music producer

"Music will not save your spot. Often, that's the beginning of the conference call: 'We really think music can save this'. No, it can't! Music can reinforce the story you're trying to tell and point you in an emotional direction, but it's not going to save your spot."
Keith Haluska (1971), managing director Massive Music NY

TAKE RISKS

rule 33

Playing it safe will only get you so far in life. No guts, no glory.

"Do the next thing."
John Wanamaker (1838-1922), American businessman

"Playing it safe can be the most dangerous thing in the world, because you're presenting people with an idea they've seen before, and you won't have impact."
Bill Bernbach (1911-1982), American advertising executive

"Of course, I'm a legend. But it's not because of any great gift I have. It's because I'm a risk taker."
Mary Wells Lawrence (1928), American advertising executive

"Taking risks gives me energy."
Jay Chiat (1931-2002), American advertising designer

"I like it when advertising does not look like advertising. Advertising is always the same – you have a beautiful photograph and then you have a text on it, and then you have a logo in the bottom. Now it is a good time to change that. The best advertising is advertising which doesn't look like other advertising."
Erik Kessels (1966), Dutch advertising executive

"Fear is the mortal enemy of creativity."
Alex Bogusky (1963), American advertising executive

rule 34

If you can't fix it, feature it!

If you can't hide it, make a feature out of it. The best example is Kesselskramer's widely-applauded campaign for Hans Brinker Budget Hotel, which highlighted the worst aspects of this Amsterdam dive, with slogans like 'Now even more noise!', 'Now even less service!' and 'Now even more dog shit in the main entrance!'

"The Budget Hotel is something I am quite proud of… It is such a bad hotel but then only by the communication we do we doubled the visits. We are quite proud of that."
Erik Kessels (1966), Dutch advertising executive

"It sounds counterintuitive, but admitting a negative about your company or product in your advertising builds trust with consumers."
Steve McKee (1963), American BusinessWeek.com columnist and advertising exec

"If you have a big wart on your face, you'd better make that your thing. Make people love that wart. Convince everyone it's a beauty mark. But don't waste a second trying to hide it."
Andrew Keller (1970), American advertising executive

A picture is worth a thousand words

This somewhat clichéd sentence can be traced back to 1921 when the advertising trade journal *Printers' Ink* ran an ad which read: "One Look is Worth A Thousand Words." In the ad Fred R. Barnard talked about the benefits of advertising on street cars. According to Barnard, the advertisement's headline was taken from a "famous Japanese philosopher." Six years later Barnard used the sentence in another ad, this time slightly changing it into: "One Picture is Worth Ten Thousand Words."

"One ad is worth more to a paper than forty editorials."

Will Rogers (1879-1935), American humorist

"An image is not simply a trademark, a design, a slogan or an easily remembered picture. It is a studiously crafted personality profile of an individual, institution, corporation, product or service."
Daniel J. Boorstin (1914-2004), American historian

"As the Chinese say, 1001 words are worth more than a picture."
John McCarthy (1927), American computer scientist

"A picture is worth a thousand dollars."
Marty Neumeier (1947), American communication designer, writer and publisher

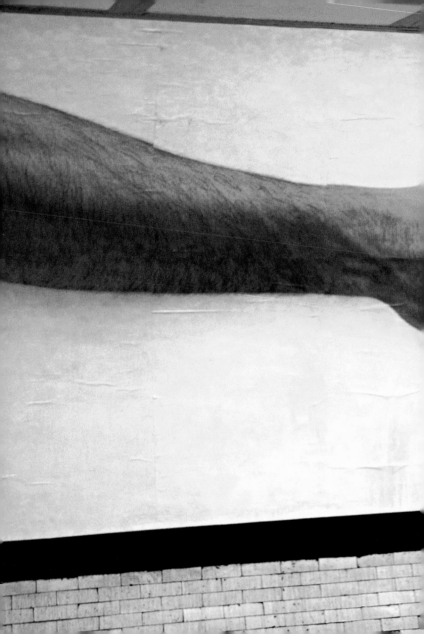

GO VIRAL

Going viral, a modern version of the old word of mouth technique, is all the rage. Viral is the future, viral means guaranteed success, viral is what the cool kids are doing. What is often forgotten is that not every cold spreads. And even if your viral does catch on, you have zero control over what happens next.

"Don't sell too hard. Viral means people send stuff to their friends, and no one wants to send a salesman over to a friend's house."
Chuck Porter (1945), American advertising executive

"A lot of advertising agencies are using viral marketing to try to spread messages online. Typically, they use games, corny contests, and bait-and-switch banner ads. It works; it spreads like a virus."
David Meerman Scott (1961), American marketing strategist

"Interruption or disruption as the fundamental premise of marketing no longer works. You have to create content that is interesting, useful or entertaining enough to invite. Viral is the ultimate invitation."
Jeff Hicks (1965), American advertising executive

"All viral means... is that you've created a message that people want to share. It's proof that your message is resonating. If people want to pass it along, that's what brand marketing is all about."
Gregg Spiridellis, co-founder of design studio JibJab

"You can't expect your messaging to stay contained within your target demographic. The information you put out will spread, and that spread is beyond your control. There are only two reasons why information doesn't spread once it is out: a) people are just uninterested in your message, b) it's in a language people don't speak, which is really just a subset of 'a', frankly."
Chris Abraham (1970), American social media marketer

"For us, viral means a great ad. Something that someone would talk about, tell their friends about, send to them. TV spots are viral, print ads are viral, internet ads are viral when they're great."
Jeff Benjamin (1975), American advertising executive

Packaging is everything

Not all customers are shallow shoppers.
Still, never underestimate the selling
power of pretty packaging.

"Well-designed packages can create convenience and promotional value. We must include packaging as a styling weapon, especially in food products, cosmetics, toiletries and small consumer appliances. The package is the buyer's first encounter with the product and is capable of turning the buyer on or off."
Philip Kotler (1931), American International Marketing professor, and Kevin Lane Keller (1950), American Marketing professor

"More and more products are coming out in fiercely protective packaging designed to prevent consumers from consuming them. These days you have to open almost every consumer item by gnawing on the packaging."
Dave Barry (1947), American humorist and author

"The media is fragmented, and we can't find people — we can't get them to sit down and listen to our argument on a television spot. The package can convey that argument."
Jerry Kathman (1953), American brand design executive

GOOD DESIGN

· · IS ALL ABOUT MAKING · ·

OTHER DESIGNERS

FEEL LIKE

IDIOTS

· · · BECAUSE THAT IDEA · · ·

WASN'T THEIRS

Life's a pitch

It's a dog eat dog world, so if you want to land that account, you'd better polish your elevator pitch and be prepared to fight off competing agencies, who are also trying to woo the potential client with campaign ideas.

"To show that I'm paying attention, I interrupt with questions during the pitch. If I know I'm going to pass I usually lay the groundwork by bringing up my concerns. If you hear me say, 'It's an interesting story but my concern is...', it's a good indication that you're toast."
Nina Jacobson (1966), American film executive

"Making a pitch is not just a matter of winning the pet-food account in an airless meeting room at one of those hotels where people conduct that sort of business. The whole of life is a pitch. Everything you do is a matter of presentation and persuasion."
Stephen Bayley and Roger Mavity, authors of Life's A Pitch *(2007)*

"I have found that an effective elevator pitch is nine things: Concise, Clear, Compelling, Credible, Conceptual, Concrete, Consistent, Customized, Conversational."
Chris O'Leary, American author of Elevator Pitch Essentials *(2008)*

Make your name stick

What's in a name? Well, in the world of advertising a whole lot. In 2005 Dutch beer brand Shag was banned in Australia because of its rather raunchy advertising slogan 'Fancy a Shag?' Mr. Grant McBride, then Gaming and Racing Minister, initiated the ban: "I'm outraged by this product. To name the product Shag links it directly with sexual intercourse – and that's not on." Never mind that the beer was named after the cormorant bird which was also featured on the Shag label.

"There is great advantage in a name that tells a story. The name is usually prominently displayed. To justify the space it occupies, it should aid the advertising. Some such names are almost complete advertisements in themselves. May Breath is such a name. Cream of Wheat is another. That name alone has been worth a fortune."
Claude C. Hopkins (1866-1932), American advertising pioneer

HELLO
MY NAME IS

HELLO
MY NAME IS

"The proper term for manufacturing a name is a 'neologism'. Anybody with a computer or a set of Scrabble tiles can crank out a newly-minted word like Anadem or Zixoryn. But the trick is to create a new name that is meaningful, impactful and starts the positioning process for the brand or company."
Steve Rivkin (1947), American marketing and communications consultant

"Brand names are a part of the soundtracks of our lives – some by chance, some on purpose... Words owned by corporations have become core components of our modern language, if not a new language entirely, seeping into vernacular speech. Instead of drinking a cup of coffee, increasingly we 'get Starbucks'. We 'do the StairMaster'. We FedEx packages, take an Advil, and apply ChapStick."
Alex Frankel (1970), American writer and brand observer

Be original

Try to be original. And if that fails, make sure you steal from the best.

"The secret of all effective originality in advertising is not the creation of new and tricky words and pictures, but one of putting familiar words and pictures into new relationships."
Leo Burnett (1891-1971), American advertising executive

"Creativity often consists merely of turning up what is already there. Did you know that right and left shoes were thought up only a little more than a century ago?"
Bernice Fitz-Gibbon (1894-1982), American advertising executive

"Already been done doesn't work. 'Imitation can be commercial suicide'."
Bill Bernbach (1911-1982), American advertising executive

"Sometimes there is simply no need to be either clever or original."

Ivan Chermayeff (1932), American graphic designer

"Forget words like 'hard sell' and 'soft sell.' That will only confuse you. Just be sure your advertising is saying something with substance, something that will inform and serve the consumer, and be sure you're saying it like it's never been said before."
Bill Bernbach (1911-1982), American advertising executive

"Originality is a product, not an intention."
Paul Rand (1914-1996), American graphic designer

"To achieve originality we need to abandon the comforts of habit, reason, and the approval of our peers."
Marty Neumeier (1947), American communication designer, writer and publisher

"Originality is non-existent."
Jim Jarmusch (1953), American filmmaker

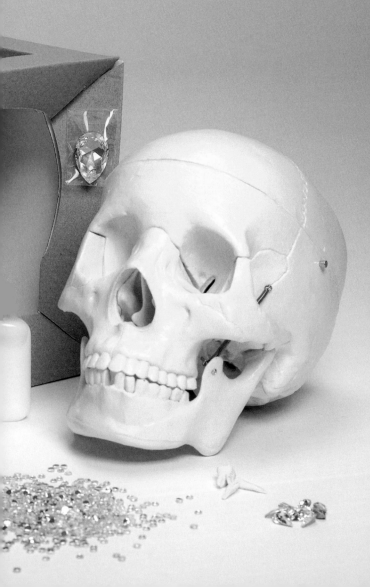

Treat competitors fairly

It's tempting to knock the competition, but it's like your grandmother used to say: "If you can't say anything nice, don't say anything at all." Negative campaigning is a no-no.

"The competitor to be feared is one who never bothers about you at all, but goes on making his own business better all the time."
Henry Ford (1863-1947), American businessman

"If any of my competitors were drowning, I'd stick a hose in their mouth."
Ray Kroc (1902-1984), American businessman of McDonalds fame

"Many manufacturers secretly question whether advertising really sells their product, but are vaguely afraid that their competitors might steal a march on them if they stopped."
David Ogilvy (1911-1999), British advertising executive

"Marketers of consumer products, borrowing a page from the electoral playbook, are becoming more willing to run aggressive ads in which brands attack their competitors by name. A major reason for the growing popularity of such ads is the faltering economy, on the theory that when times are hard, you should hit your opponent harder."
Stuart Elliott (1952), American advertising columnist of The New York Times

"Whether it's Google or Apple or free software, we've got some fantastic competitors and it keeps us on our toes."
Bill Gates (1955), American businessman

"ADVERTISING IS LEGALIZED LYING."

rule 42

"Advertising is legalized lying," said English author H. G. Wells (1866-1946), which makes him a true visionary to some and a major cynic to others.

"What is the difference between unethical and ethical advertising? Unethical advertising uses falsehoods to deceive the public; ethical advertising uses truth to deceive the public."
Vilhjalmur Stefansson (1879-1962), Canadian explorer

"Regardless of the moral issue, dishonesty in advertising has proved very unprofitable."
Leo Burnett (1891-1971), American advertising executive

"You can fool all the people all the time if the advertising is right and the budget is big enough."
Joseph E. Levine (1905-1987), American movie producer

"Telling lies does not work in advertising."
Stanislaw Lec (1909-1966), Polish poet

"The most powerful element in advertising is the truth."
Bill Bernbach (1911-1982), American advertising executive

"Political advertising ought to be stopped. It's the only really dishonest kind of advertising that's left. It's totally dishonest."
David Ogilvy (1911-1999), British advertising executive

"Simple commercial messages, pushed through whatever medium, in order to reach a potential customer who is in the middle of doing something else, will fail. It's not that we no longer need information to initiate or to complete a transaction; rather, we will no longer need advertising to obtain that information. We will see the information we want, when we want it, from sources that we trust more than paid advertising."
Eric K. Clemons (1948), American Professor of Operations and Information Management

"There is a huge difference between journalism and advertising. Journalism aspires to truth. Advertising is regulated for truth. I'll put the accuracy of the average ad in this country up against the average news story any time."
Jef I. Richards (1955), American advertising professor

"To effectively 'hype' something today, you must find a way to cut through 'the hype'. Strange as it might seem in advertising, this necessitates telling the truth – or at least some interesting form of it. It is not as easy as it might sound, because advertisers, promoters, and publicists have, for decades, developed a habit of relying on overpromising, overselling, and focusing on the sizzle instead of the steak."
Warren Berger (1958), American writer and journalist

"You're a liar. So am I. Everyone is a liar. We tell ourselves stories because we're superstitious. Stories are shortcuts we use because we're too overwhelmed by data to discover all the details. The stories we tell ourselves are lies that make it far easier to live in a very complicated world. We tell stories about products, services, friends, job seekers, the New York Yankees and sometimes even the weather."
Seth Godin (1960), American marketing expert and author of All Marketers Are Liars

"Brands that are unwilling to have a real and truthful conversation with consumers will become completely irrelevant and therefore invisible."
Alex Bogusky (1963), American advertising executive

THI

BULL

FREE

S A

SHIT ZONE.

Sell! Sell!

Advertising is art

According to Canadian communication theorist Marshall 'The Medium is the Message' McLuhan (1911–1980) "advertising is the greatest art form of the 20th century." Pretty bold statement that is bound to raise more than a few eyebrows. Still, you've got to agree that there is an art to creating good ads or convincing people to go out and buy product X over Y.

"Advertising is the art of convincing people to spend money they don't have for something they don't need."
Will Rogers (1879-1935), American humorist

"Ads are the cave art of the twentieth century."
Marshall McLuhan (1911–1980), Canadian communication theorist

"Advertising is fundamentally persuasion and persuasion happens to be not a science, but an art."
Bill Bernbach (1911-1982), American advertising executive

"I do not regard advertising as entertainment or an art form, but as a medium of information."
David Ogilvy (1911-1999), British advertising executive

"Advertising is not a fucking science. Advertising is an art – no questions about it."
George Lois (1931), American advertising executive

"If advertising is not an official or state art, it is nonetheless clearly art."
Michael Schudson (1946), American sociologist

"I believe in advertisement and media completely. My art and my personal life are based in it. I think that the art world would probably be a tremendous reservoir for everybody involved in advertising."
Jeff Koons (1955), American artist

"Creative without strategy is called 'art'. Creative with strategy is called 'advertising'."
Jef I. Richards (1955), American advertising professor

"People have romantic notions about television. In the highest realms they think it's some sort of art medium, and it's not. Others think it's an entertainment medium, it's not that either. It's an advertising medium. It's a method to deliver advertising like a cigarette is a method to deliver nicotine."
Bill Maher (1956), American comedian

When times are good, advertise.
When times are tough, advertise more

Dropping sales figures, shrinking advertising budgets, bad publicity or a global recession. When the going gets tough, the advertiser had better get creative.

———

"In good times, people want to advertise; in bad times, they have to."
Bruce Barton (1886-1967), American author and advertising executive

"During boom times, no one can be heard above the din. In slower times, anyone with a creative message will stand out – and gain an advantage on competitors who have gone quiet."
Philip Kotler (1931), American International Marketing professor, and Kevin Lane Keller (1950), American Marketing professor

"In rough times, advertisers are in need of creative agencies with new, bold ideas and the imagination to connect and reach consumers."
Maurice Lévy (1942), French advertising executive

"In times of recession, that's when good companies innovate and invest... To use a good Canadian euphemism, they're skating to where the puck is going to be."
Patrick Pichette, Canadian Senior Vice President and CFO Google

"When we see a recession, and we've been through a few now, and when we see the industry pull back, we always think that's an opportunity, because there are a lot of people that just use that as an excuse to not work that hard. They say, 'Ok, everything's bad, we've got nothing going on and we'll call it in for a while'."
Alex Bogusky (1963), American advertising executive

 **Closing Out Sale**

Advertising
is obsolete

rule
45

As long as there are products to push and services to sell, there will be a need for some sort of advertising.

_____

"I can't say the advertising model is obsolete yet but it doesn't make a lot of sense in the long range."
Jay Chiat (1931-2002), American advertising designer

"Sometimes I feel as though I am standing at the graveside of a well-loved friend called advertising."
Maurice Saatchi (1946), Iraqi-born British advertising executive

"The game is more interesting and more relevant than ever."
Shelly Lazarus (born 1947), American advertising executive

"My basic premise is that the internet is not replacing advertising but shattering it, and all the king's horses, all the king's men, and all the creative talent of Madison Avenue cannot put it together again."
Eric K. Clemons (1948), American Professor of Operations and Information Management

"Building a relationship between a brand and the consumer requires more and different touch points. Advertising is not less important; it's just that other communications tools are becoming more important. That said, advertising will probably remain the primary tool in the future."
John Dooner (1948), American advertising executive

"The Death of Advertising? I think that's in the book of Revelation. It's the day when people everywhere become satisfied with their weight, their hair, their skin, their wardrobe, and their aroma."
Jef I. Richards (1955), American advertising professor

"Today, the average American receives more than 3,000 marketing messages a day, and I would argue that advertising has never been more relevant. As people's attention spans shorten, there's an even greater need for an enduring brand. Of course, the challenge is creating campaigns that will last a decade. The future of advertising lies with passionate brand advocates who not only bring ideas to their clients but also help them figure out how to communicate those ideas in a truly integrated way."
Dawn Hudson (1958), American advertising executive

"The future of advertising is that there isn't any."
Jeff Hicks (1965), American advertising executive

delete

THE EASY
WAY TO
PAY BILLS

LA PRÓXIMA
VEZ, AHORRE
TIEMPO, PAGUE
SUS CUENTAS
AQUÍ.

If it doesn't sell, it isn't creative

Contrary to what you might think, this book is not (just) an ode to Ogilvy. Yes, he has been quoted more than any other ad man. But that's only because the world of advertising owes many of its rules to the British advertising exec, and the above-mentioned rule is no exception.

"I am one who believes that one of the greatest dangers of advertising is not that of misleading people, but that of boring them to death."
Leo Burnett (1891-1971), American advertising executive

"When I write an advertisement, I don't want you to tell me that you find it 'creative'. I want you to find it so interesting that you buy the product."
David Ogilvy (1911-1999), British advertising executive

"Creativity is an advertising agency's most valuable asset, because it is the rarest. "
Jef I. Richards (1955), American advertising professor

"If ad agencies are truly in the idea business, then they need to shed completely the old mentality of simply making ads. They're beginning to turn in that direction, which is actually a return to what the industry has always been about: creativity."
Dawn Hudson (1958), American advertising executive

k is for

boys

Direct mail isn't dead (just yet)

In a high-tech world direct mail might seem like an archaic form of advertising, but take one look at the amount of brochures, flyers, and other unsolicited promotional material that awaits us on the doormat everyday and it becomes clear that direct mail is still alive and kicking.

"Direct mail is a popular medium because it permits target market selectivity, can be personalized, is flexible, and allows early testing and response measurement. Although the cost per thousand people reached is higher than with mass media, the people reached are much better prospects."

Philip Kotler (1931), American International Marketing professor, and Kevin Lane Keller (1950), American Marketing professor

"It is hard to imagine waste more unnecessary than the 100 billion pieces of junk mail Americans receive each year."

Dr. James Hansen (1941), American climate scientist

"The Internet has actually been a trigger of direct mail. With every company now basically having a customer-facing website, suddenly they're having an interactivity with their customers that is much more real to them."
Peter A. Johnson, American vice president Direct Marketing Association

"It's hard to argue against any well-intentioned effort to use more recycled paper, but the idea of greening junk mail is still a bit like putting lipstick on a pig."
Todd J. Paglia, American director nonprofit organization ForestEthics

"Chances are, direct mail is one of the most effective tools your organization can use to build your base in the century ahead. But you can do so only by using a creative, no-holds-barred, entrepreneurial approach to direct mail, making use of the newest insights and the latest technologies to gain maximum advantage for your organization."
Mal Warwick, American author Revolution in the Mailbox: Your Guide to Successful Direct Mail Fundraising (2004)

Determine the medium that works best for your business... and dominate it

The savvy marketer knows that you first have to determine the medium that works best for your business and then go in for the kill, i.e. dominate it.

―――――――

"Digital is a new world and we should not compare digital to what digital was in 2000. In 2000 digital was mainly websites and some funny things and obviously when the market collapsed, everything collapsed. Today there is the Google of the world, there is the Yahoo of the world, and the MSN and we are all looking for addressing the communication to the end users through search and through different ways of communication. And this communication is highly measured – we know if it is working or not, we know the return on investment immediately, we know what works and what doesn't work."
Maurice Lévy (1942), French advertising executive

"You will thrive going forward because you embrace the new forms of communication, not because you turn your nose up at them."
Seth Godin (1960), American marketing expert

"People are often focused on figuring out if the next advertising medium will be via the Internet, TiVo, or some technological device we don't even know about yet. In my mind, the future of advertising is in great brands that market themselves without paid advertising."
Jeff Hicks (1965), American advertising executive

"You can't do all kinds of media. Own something. You can feel a little bit bigger in your own little realm."
Andrew Keller (1970), American advertising executive

Get celebrities to endorse your product

Having some A-list actor or gifted golf player publicly endorse your product might seem like a good idea and there are plenty of excellent examples of celebrity endorsement, but beware, not all celebs make for good salesmen.

"The choice of the celebrity is critical. The celebrity should have high recognition, high positive affect, and high appropriateness to the product."
Philip Kotler (1931), American International Marketing professor, and Kevin Lane Keller (1950), American Marketing professor

"Incidents, and the damage-control efforts they require, have always plagued marketers. Remember Pepsi-Cola's embarrassment when it was revealed that Michael Jackson never touches Pepsi? Or the Beef Industry Council's dismay when James Garner underwent heart surgery?"
Stuart Elliott (1952), American advertising columnist of The New York Times

"Celebrity spokespeople are expensive and risky, and they don't always pay off. If you believe your brand is in need of additional equity, instead of borrowing it from a celebrity, develop it yourself… Take the money you would otherwise hand over to an already well-paid celebrity and invest it in developing original creative ideas that will make your brand stand out. That way, the equity you create will be nothing but your own."
Steve McKee (1963), American BusinessWeek.com columnist and advertising exec

"Celebrity endorsements only work when the consumer has a credible belief that the celebrity would be interested in buying and using your product or service despite being paid to do so."
Laura Ries (1971), American marketing expert

hear
ffy's
lling
ke."

dr:d

Be believable

Have an idea. Make it memorable. Keep it simple. Be believable. The rules of advertising are as short and catchy as they are dogmatic.

———

"The greatest thing to be achieved in advertising, in my opinion, is believability, and nothing is more believable than the product itself."
Leo Burnett (1891-1971), American advertising executive

"In the end, branding is about...
CREDIBILITY."
Tom Peters (1942), American management consultant

"Advertising relies on stereotypes because it has to tell a story through a single image, or in just 30 seconds. Business people always wear suits and carry briefcases, construction workers have northern accents and checked shirts. It's a form of shorthand to have a granddad with specs, grey hair and wearing a cardi, and I see nothing wrong with that. Whether that stereotype is subsequently denigrated is a different matter."
Tess Alps (1953), British TV marketing executive

"Tiger Woods endorsing the Buick brand makes no sense at all. There is just no believability that Tiger is dying to drive a Buick. And without believability a celebrity endorsement is worthless."
Laura Ries (1971), American marketing expert

BE HONEST

TO YOURSELF.
TO YOUR AUDIENCE.

BREAK THE RULES

rule
51

Now that you've read all the rules, feel free to break them.

———

"Rules are what the artist breaks; the memorable never emerged from a formula."
Bill Bernbach (1911-1982), American advertising executive

"I am sometimes attacked for imposing 'rules'. Nothing could be further from the truth. I hate rules. All I do is report on how consumers react to different stimuli."
David Ogilvy (1911-1999), British advertising executive

"The only quality I really have an appreciation for is newness. To see something no one's ever seen before. New comes at 11 o'clock at night when you've spent a day hunched over the board. New means breaking rules."
Helmut Krone (1925-1996), American art director

"If you can't solve a problem, it's because you're playing by the rules."
Paul Arden (1940-2008), British advertising executive and author

"The old rules no longer apply when it comes to communicating effectively, building a brand, making something famous, or creating a cultural phenomenon of any type... Most were created for another era, when there was less noise, less hype, less technology; a time when the people you might be trying to communicate with were easier to reach and influence – before they developed advanced mutant powers enabling them to sort, filter, manipulate or just ignore information."
Warren Berger (1958), American writer and journalist

CONTRIBUTORS

1 Petter Buhagen
(www.petterbuhagen.com)

2 iri5
(www.iri5.com)

3 Ryan Chapman
(www.ryan-chapman.com)

4 Matt Stuart
(www.mattstuart.com)

5 Hartog & Henneman
(www.hartoghenneman.com)

6 LOVE.
(www.lovecreative.com)

7 Lennart Wolfert
(www.lennartwolfert.nl)

8 Tuomas Ikonen
(www.tuomasikonen.com)

9 Javier Gutierrez (cc)
(www.flickr.com/photos/javigutierrez)

10 Melanie Bell
(www.melbell.etsy.com)

11 Nicole Schulze
(www.nicoleschulze.com)

12 Sam LeVan

13 Frank Uyttenhove
(www.frankuyttenhove.com)

14 Liliana Ospina
(www.lilondra.com)

15 Frederique Daubal
(www.daubal.com)

16 Brock Davis
(www.itistheworldthatmadeyousmall.com)

17 Photographer: Rob Sullivan (cc)
(www.flickr.com/photos/ro_jo_sul)

- Artist: dr. d
(www.drd.mu)

18 DTM_INC
(dtm_inc@hotmail.com)

19 Sean Aikins (cc)
(www.flickr.com/photos/codezero)

20 Jeff Sheldon
(www.ugmonk.com)

21 William Dohman
(www.williamdohman.etsy.com)

22 Nate Duval
(www.nateduval.com)

23 Danyllo Queiroz (cc)
(www.flickr.com/photos/nyllows)

24 Andrew Magill (cc)
(www.ominoushum.com)

25 Illegal Art
(www.illegalart.org)

26 Robert Hunter
(www.rob-hunter.co.uk)

27 Lianne van de Laar
(www.photographicsby.com)

28 Denise van Leeuwen
(www.denisevanleeuwen.com)

29 Photography: Maurice Scheltens
(www.mauricescheltens.com)

- Freestyling: Wilfried Nijhof

- Art Direction: Jop van Bennekom

Taken from Re-Magazine, 2000

30 KesselsKramer
(www.kesselskramer.com)

- Illustrator: Anthony Burrill

31 Matt Robinson
(www.matthewrobinson.co.uk)

- Tom Wrigglesworth
(www.tomwrigglesworth.com)

32 Art Director: Carter Storozynski
& Trevor Bittinger
(www.trevorbittinger.com)

- Copywriter: Alex Taylor

33 Zoe More O'Ferrall
(www.zoemof.com)

34 Naroa Lizar Redrado
(www.iartistlondon.com)

- Photographer: Erno-Erik Raitanen
(www.ernoraitanen.com)

35 Anne de Vries
(www.annedevries.info)

36 Thomas Duesing
(www.tfduesing.net)

37 Frank Chimero
(www.frankchimero.com)

38 Ji Lee (cc)
(www.pleaseenjoy.com)

39 Sell! Sell!
(www.sellsell.co.uk)

40 Stuart Bannocks (cc)
(www.stuartbannocks.co.uk)

41 Bryan Partington (cc)
(www.striatic.net)

INDEX BY SUBJECT

INDEX BY NAME

Thanks to:
Premsela, Dutch Platform for Design and Fashion (www.premsela.org)
Lemon Scented Tea (www.lemonscentedtea.com)